DATE DUE

PRINTED IN U.S.A.

Let's Get Mapping!

Mapping the World

Melanie Waldron

Chicago, Illinois

Edited by Nancy Dickmann and Abby Colich
Designed by Victoria Allen
Original illustrations © 2013
Illustrated by HL Studios
Picture research by Ruth Blair
Originated by Capstone Global Library Limited
Printed and bound in China by CTPS

17 16 15 14 13 12
10 9 8 7 6 5 4 3 2 1

**Library of Congress Cataloging-in-Publication
Data**
Waldron, Melanie.
  Mapping the world / Melanie Waldron.
      p. cm.—(Let's get mapping!)
  Includes bibliographical references and index.
  ISBN 978-1-4109-4903-5 (hb)—ISBN 978-1-4109-
4910-3 (pb) 1. Cartography—Juvenile literature.
2. World maps—Juvenile literature. I. Title.
  GA105.6.W343 2012b
  526—dc23   2012008516

Acknowledgments

We would like to thank the following for
permission to reproduce photographs:
Alamy: pp. 5 (© Mark Gibson), 25 (© NASA
Images), 26 (© Stockbroker), 27 (© Bob
Daemmrich); © Capstone Publishers: p. 29
(Karon Dubke); Corbis: pp. 10 (© Ocean),
15 (© NARONG SANGNAK/epa), 20 (© MAPS.
com), 24 (© NASA); Photoshot: p. 13 (© UPPA);
Science Photo Library: p. 18 (DYNAMIC EARTH
IMAGING); Shutterstock: pp. 11 (© Matt Cooper),
16 (© Sam DCruz), 22 (© andrej pol); Superstock:
pp. 4 (© Fancy Collection), 6 (© Gallo Images),
23 (© age footstock).

Cover photograph of a boy pointing to a globe
reproduced with permission from Shutterstock
(© wavebreakmedia ltd).

Background images and design features
reproduced with permission from Shutterstock.

Contents

Some words appear in the text in bold, **like this**. You can find out what they mean by looking in the glossary.

Maps and Mapmakers

A map is usually a flat piece of paper showing some information about the land. Most maps show a "bird's-eye view" of the land. This means that they show how the land looks from above.

Maps can show lots of different information. They can show Earth's **natural features**, such as volcanoes and rivers. They can also show things that humans have built on the land, such as factories and roads. Maps are really useful for seeing how an area has changed over time.

People use maps to help them understand places and locations.

What are maps used for?

Maps of the world are useful for lots of things. Television news reports or newspaper stories about different countries often have world maps showing where these countries are. When we learn about different countries, it is helpful to see where these countries are compared to our own. World maps can show us countries that are close to us and countries that are very far from us.

MAPMAKERS

People who make maps are called **cartographers**. Making maps is called cartography.

Mapping a Globe

Earth is not flat. Instead it is a **sphere**—a round object, like a ball. Using a **globe** is the best way to look at a map of the world. All the countries and oceans are in exactly the right places on a globe.

There are some problems with using globes. They are difficult to carry around and store. You cannot put globes inside books or newspapers. They are also usually more expensive than paper maps.

Using a globe is a good way to understand where different **continents** and countries are.

Flattened Earth

Flat maps are much easier to use than globes. When we look at flat maps of the world, we have to try to remember that the real world is a sphere. Cartographers use special ways of drawing to get all of the countries on to the flat paper. They have to stretch some areas, and squeeze other areas, to get everything to fit.

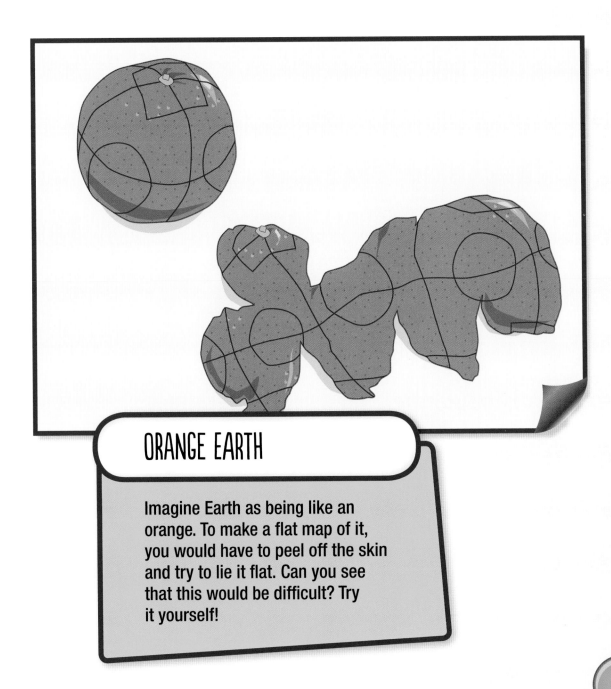

ORANGE EARTH

Imagine Earth as being like an orange. To make a flat map of it, you would have to peel off the skin and try to lie it flat. Can you see that this would be difficult? Try it yourself!

Stretching the World

Many flat maps of the world try to show the correct shape of the land. This means that the sizes are often not correct. Maps that use a Mercator **Projection** have this problem. A projection is a way of showing a solid object on a flat surface.

Mercator Projection maps were first made in 1569. They show the shapes of the land, but the sizes are not accurate. Greenland looks almost as big as South America, when in fact South America is around eight times bigger!

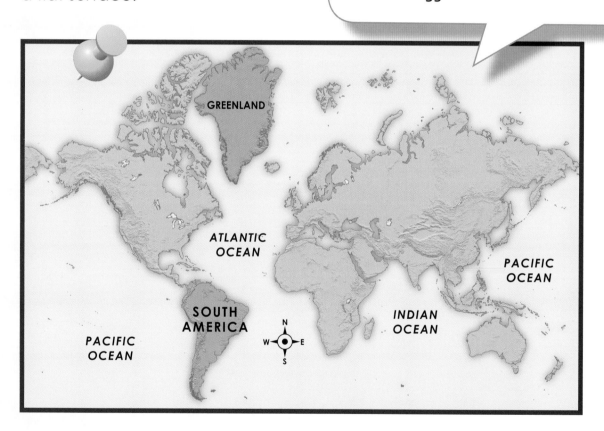

GREENLAND

ATLANTIC
OCEAN

PACIFIC
OCEAN

SOUTH
AMERICA

PACIFIC
OCEAN

INDIAN
OCEAN

N
W — E
S

Some cartographers have tried to make the land sizes more accurate. This means that the shapes have to be stretched. In 1885, James Gall created a map that showed the correct land sizes. In 1974, this became known as the Peters Projection, or sometimes the Gall-Peters Projection.

WINKEL-TRIPEL

In 1921, Oswald Winkel found a new way to show a world map. He tried to balance the problems of size and shape. This way of showing the world is used by many people now.

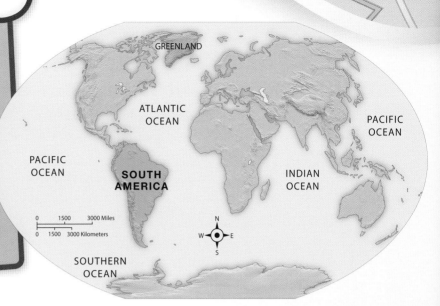

This is a Peters Projection world map. The sizes are more accurate—South America is much bigger than Greenland. But can you see how the shapes of the land masses have been stretched?

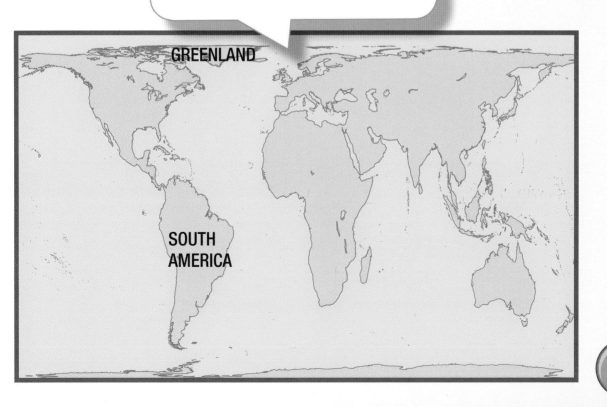

Lines Around the World

Many world maps have lines running across and down them. Lines of **latitude** are imaginary lines that go around Earth. They are sometimes called parallels. The **equator** is the line of latitude known as 0 degrees. The North Pole is at 90 degrees North, and the South Pole is at 90 degrees South.

Lines of **longitude** run from the top to the bottom of Earth. They are sometimes called meridians. The **prime meridian** is the line at 0 degrees. All the others lines are east or west of the prime meridian.

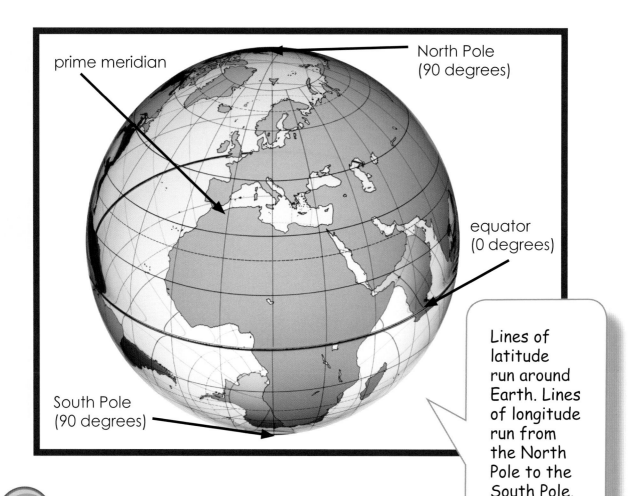

prime meridian

North Pole
(90 degrees)

equator
(0 degrees)

South Pole
(90 degrees)

Lines of latitude run around Earth. Lines of longitude run from the North Pole to the South Pole.

Using the lines

Cartographers use lines of latitude and longitude to help them make flat maps of the world. By checking the positions of the lines on a globe, they can make sure that countries are placed correctly next to each other.

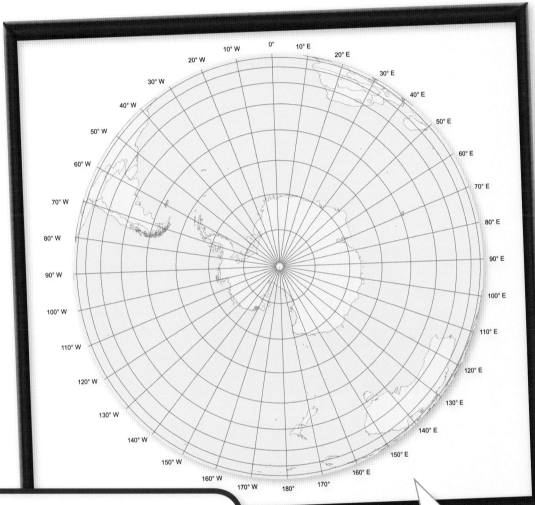

FLAT EARTH

Over 2,000 years ago, most people thought Earth was flat. Then the ancient Greeks guessed that it must be a sphere. They were proven correct when explorers sailed around the world for the first time in 1519–22.

All lines of longitude meet at the South Pole (shown here) and the North Pole.

Pinpointing Places

Finding places on Earth's surface is easier than you might think. We can use lines of latitude and longitude to give each place its own **coordinates**. Coordinates are made up of two numbers. The first is how many degrees of latitude the place is north or south of the equator. The second is the degrees of longitude east or west of the prime meridian.

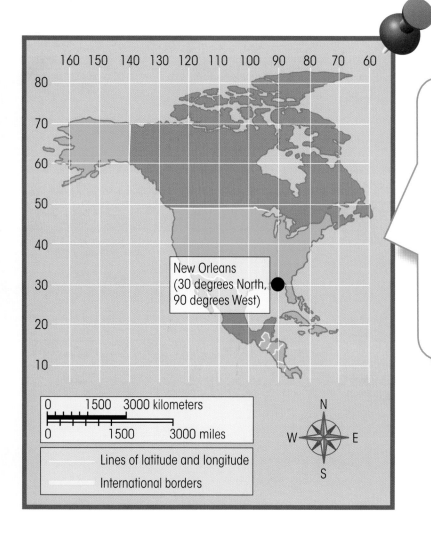

New Orleans
(30 degrees North,
90 degrees West)

0 1500 3000 kilometers

0 1500 3000 miles

—— Lines of latitude and longitude

······ International borders

N
W   E
S

This map of North America shows latitude and longitude lines. The city of New Orleans is located at 30 degrees North, 90 degrees West. These are its coordinates.

Between the lines

Places that do not lie on an exact line of latitude or longitude can still have coordinates. The distances between each line are split into 60 minutes. For example, Madrid, in Spain, has coordinates of 40 degrees and 10 minutes North, 3 degrees and 30 minutes West.

THE POLES

At the North and South Poles, all the lines of longitude meet up. This means that the coordinates are simply 90 degrees North for the North Pole, and 90 degrees South for the South Pole. There is a marker at the South Pole. These flags are at the South Pole.

The Political World

Some maps of the world are political maps. Political maps show all the countries and the **borders** between them. Borders are usually imaginary lines separating two countries. Sometimes borders follow natural features, such as rivers or mountain ranges.

There can be borders inside countries, too. Maps of different states, regions, or counties in a country can show the borders between them. Borders help people to understand which areas are under the control of which organizations and governments.

This map shows the countries that make up the continent of South America and some of its major cities.

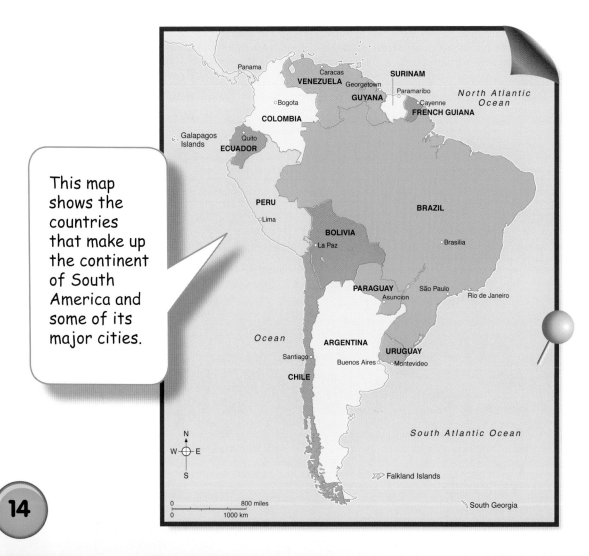

TWO HALVES

The world can be split into two halves, called **hemispheres**. The top half, north of the equator, is called the Northern Hemisphere. The bottom half, south of the equator, is called the Southern Hemisphere.

Unclear borders

Sometimes not everyone agrees about the borders between countries. These are known as disputed borders. Countries on either side want to move the border and claim more land. There is often fighting at these borders to try to settle which country owns the land.

These residents of Thailand protest in Bangkok over the disputed border with Cambodia.

The Physical World

Many world maps show the natural features of the land. These are called physical maps. They show things like major rivers and lakes, mountains and mountain ranges, and other land features such as deserts. They often ignore countries and their borders and instead just try to show what the land is like.

Some physical maps use color to show the height of the land. The lowest land is often colored green. This changes to yellow, then orange, then brown, then purple as land gets higher. Very high areas, such as the tops of mountains, are sometimes shown in white.

The world's highest mountains are the Himalayas, in Asia.

Symbols

Some physical maps use **symbols** to show where certain natural features are. Symbols are little pictures or drawings. They represent things in real life. For example, a symbol of a tree might represent a forest. Maps using symbols also usually have a **key**. The key lists all the symbols and explains what each one represents.

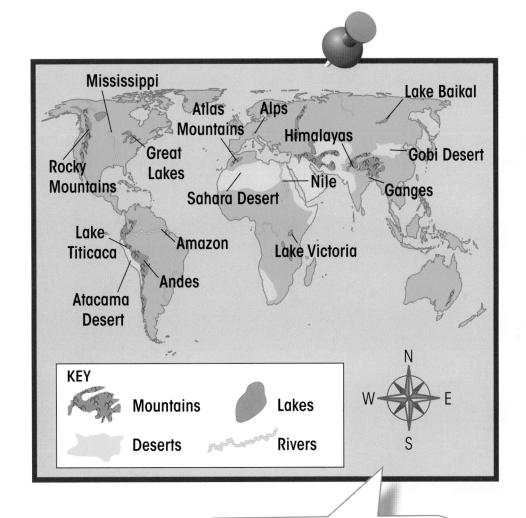

KEY

Mountains   Lakes

Deserts   Rivers

N   W   E   S

This map of the world uses symbols to show where different natural features are. Can you see the huge area of the Sahara Desert?

Water World

Mapping the world does not just mean mapping the land! Around 70 percent of Earth's surface is covered in ocean. Is it important to have maps of the ocean as well as the land. Sailors need to know how deep the sea is, so that they can steer their ships safely. Lots of the world's oil and gas comes from rocks under the sea, so oil and gas companies need to know where these rocks are.

This map shows the shape of the ocean floor around the world. Can you see that the ocean floor is not flat?

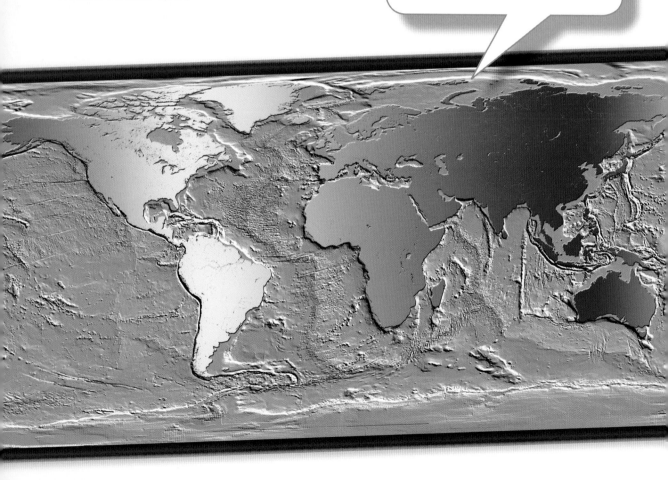

Ocean currents

The shape of the ocean floor can affect **ocean currents** around the world. Ocean currents are huge, moving bodies of water that flow in the same direction. They can be warm or cold, and they can affect the weather around the world. Maps can show the movement of these currents.

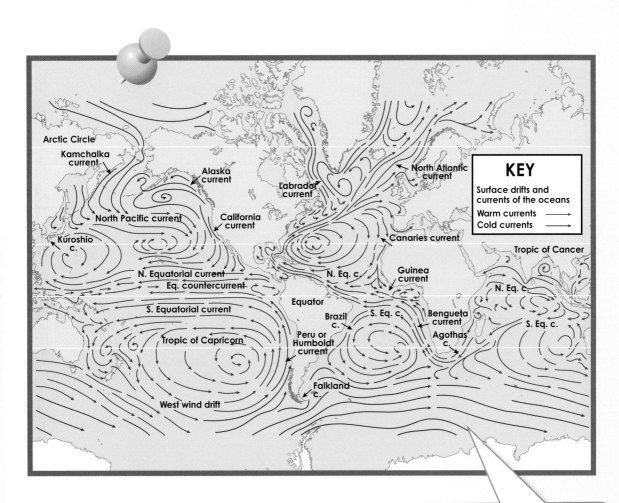

Arctic Circle

Kamchatka current

Alaska current

Labrador current

North Atlantic current

North Pacific current

California current

Kuroshio c.

Canaries current

Tropic of Cancer

N. Equatorial current

Eq. countercurrent

N. Eq. c.

Guinea current

N. Eq. c.

S. Equatorial current

Equator

Brazil c.

S. Eq. c.

Bengueta current

S. Eq. c.

Tropic of Capricorn

Peru or Humboldt current

Agothas c.

West wind drift

Falkland c.

KEY

Surface drifts and currents of the oceans

Warm currents ⟶

Cold currents ⟶

This map shows how warm and cold ocean currents move around the world. These currents can affect the weather.

SEABED CHARTS

Sailors use detailed maps of the seabed, called charts, to make sure that their ships can move safely through the water. This prevents them from becoming grounded on rocks or sand banks.

How Much Detail?

Maps cannot be as big as the area of land they are showing. Everything on a map is scaled down, or shrunk. World maps shrink everything down by a huge amount—the whole world is shown on one piece of paper! Other maps shrink everything a bit less. They might show a country or a city. They can show more detail.

This map of Canada shows more detail than a world map could show. You could use this to plan a road trip around the country.

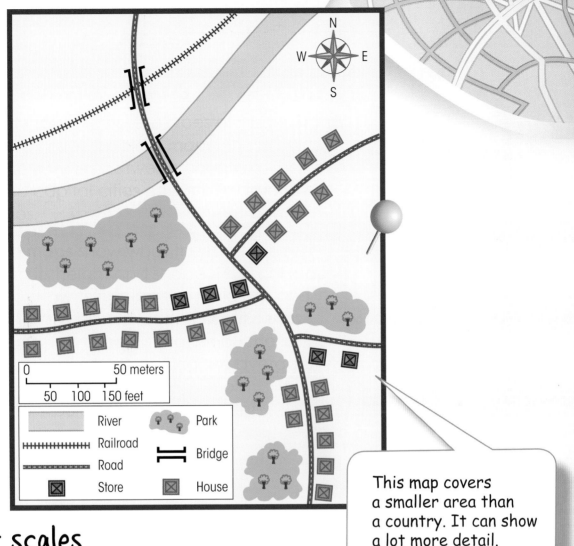

Legend:
- River
- Railroad
- Road
- Store
- Park
- Bridge
- House

Bar scale:
0 — 50 meters
50 100 150 feet

This map covers a smaller area than a country. It can show a lot more detail.

Bar scales

Some maps have a bar scale printed on them. This is a line or bar with numbers on it. You can measure something on the map and hold it against the bar scale to see how far something is in real life.

CHANGING SCALES

You will remember that it is difficult to show a sphere, like Earth, on a flat surface. The land has to be pulled and stretched to make the countries fit. Because of this pulling and stretching, world maps do not usually have a bar scale. This is because the amount of pulling and stretching is not even across the map. The bar scale would not be accurate for the whole map.

Old Maps

People have been making and using maps for hundreds of years. Explorers made maps when they discovered new lands. They wanted to record the places they had visited.

In the past, people used **compasses** to help them make maps. Compasses have a spinning needle that always points north, so they help to figure out directions. People also used **dividers** to figure out distances, and **sextants** to figure out latitudes.

This is called a sextant. Sailors used these to figure out how far north or south they were of the equator.

Printing maps

As explorers went further into new areas, maps became more and more important. In the 1400s, printing was invented. This meant that copies of maps could be made, and so more people could own them. The first atlases (books of maps) were published in the 1500s.

LEWIS AND CLARK

In 1803, President Thomas Jefferson sent Meriwether Lewis and William Clark to explore new U.S. territory. An important part of their mission was making maps. These maps later helped settlers find their way.

Early cartographers drew maps of the world and printed them in books.

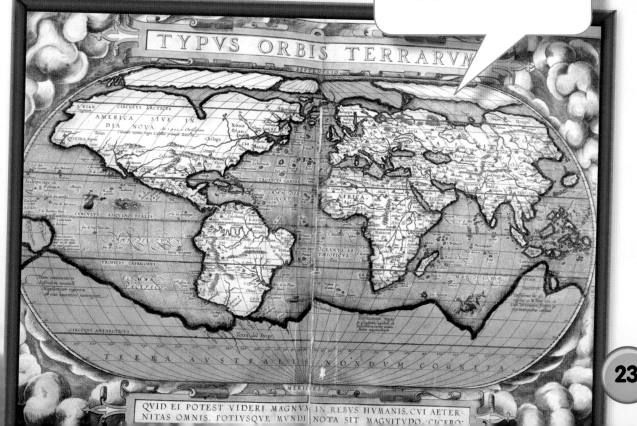

Satellites

Today, most maps of the world are made with the help of **satellites** that can take images of Earth with special cameras. This is called **remote sensing**, which means surveying something from far away.

Satellite images can show huge areas of land quickly and accurately. They can also show changes on the land surface over time. For example, the Aral Sea in Asia is shrinking, and satellite images can clearly show this.

This is a satellite image of Italy and some of its surrounding countries.

Global Positioning Systems

There are 24 Global Positioning System (GPS) satellites orbiting around Earth. They send signals to equipment called **receivers**. The receivers can figure out the exact coordinates for their positions on Earth.

Each receiver needs signals from at least three satellites to figure out the coordinates. Receivers can be very small! Some cell phones have GPS receivers built into them.

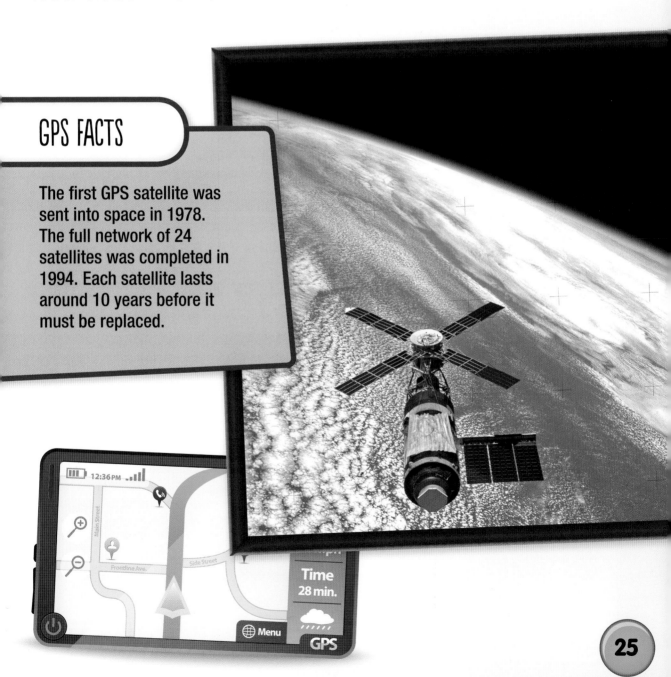

GPS FACTS

The first GPS satellite was sent into space in 1978. The full network of 24 satellites was completed in 1994. Each satellite lasts around 10 years before it must be replaced.

Using World Maps

Map reading is a really useful skill. It is important to be able to read world maps so that you can understand them and find the information you need. The first thing to do when you look at a world map is to read the map's title or caption. Then you will understand right away what it is trying to show you.

This is a globe of the world that shows South America. What do you think of when you think of a globe or world map?

Important steps in world map reading

- Try to learn roughly where your hometown or neighborhood is. It may not be marked on most world maps!

- Remember that a world map will show some areas as a bit stretched or squeezed, so they will look different on a globe.

- Stretching and squeezing also means that most world maps do not have bar scales, so do not use them to try to measure distances.

- Make sure you look at the key so that you understand what the symbols represent.

Many people like to mark all the countries that they have visited or heard about in the news on a map of the world.

Get Mapping!

You will need a globe of the world and a flat map of the world to do this activity. You will also need some string and some sticky tape.

On your flat map of the world, find the city of Toronto, in Canada. Now find the city of Nice, in France. Tape the piece of string so that it connects the cities in a straight line. Now write down all the cities that lie along this piece of string.

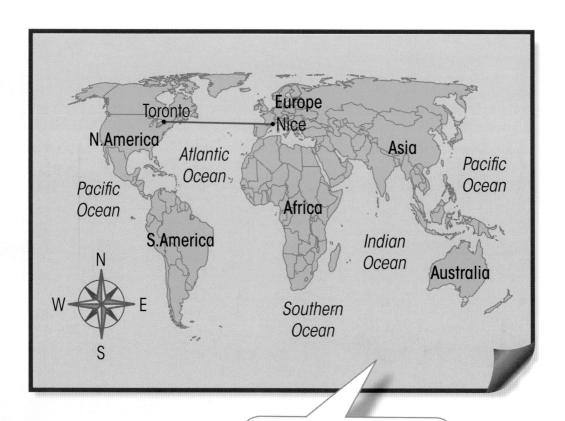

Use your flat map of the world and a piece of string to complete the above instructions.

Now find Toronto and Nice on your globe. Tape the string so that it goes from one city to another, following the shortest route around the globe. This is sometimes called a "Great Circle" route. Look at the cities the string passes through. Are they the same as the cities on the flat map?

Now compare the lengths of the string between the cities on the flat map and on the globe. Which is shorter? Why is this? Which route do you think an airplane would follow?

How does the route between the two cities on your flat map compare with the route on your globe?

Glossary

border imaginary line that separates different countries or different regions inside a country

cartographer person who makes maps

compass instrument with a needle that always points north

continent one of Earth's seven major areas of land, which are North America, South America, Europe, Africa, Asia, Australia, and Antarctica

coordinates set of numbers that show a point on a map

divider instrument used to measure distances on maps

equator imaginary circle around Earth that is halfway between the North and South Poles

globe round ball with a map of Earth on it

hemisphere one of the two halves of Earth, either above or below the equator

key list of symbols and an explanation of what each one represents

latitude distance between the equator and a point north or south on Earth's surface; this distance is measured in degrees

longitude distance on Earth's surface that is east or west of the prime meridian; this distance is usually measured in degrees

natural feature something on Earth's surface that has been created by nature—for example, a mountain

ocean current huge body of seawater that flows in the same direction and can be warm or cold

prime meridian imaginary line on Earth's surface that goes from the North Pole to the South Pole

projection way of displaying an image onto a screen or flat area

receiver instrument that receives a signal from a satellite

remote sensing surveying something from a distance rather than actually measuring it up close

satellite spacecraft that travels around Earth and gathers or sends back information

satellite image picture, like a photograph, that a satellite can take of Earth from space

sextant instrument that uses the positions of the stars to help find directions

sphere solid, round object

symbol object or picture that represents something

Find Out More

There is a whole world of maps and mapping waiting to be discovered! Start by looking at some other books and web sites.

Books

Johnson, Jinny. *Maps and Mapping* (Inside Access). Boston: Kingfisher, 2007.

Oxlade, Chris. *Global Warming* (Mapping Global Issues). Mankato, Minn.: Smart Apple Media, 2012.

Scoffham, Stephen. *School Atlas*. New York: DK, 2007.

Snedden, Robert. *Mapping Earth from Space* (Science Missions). Chicago: Raintree, 2011.

Web sites

www.nationalatlas.gov
This U.S. government web site offers many different kinds of maps of the United States. Explore the links here to learn more about maps. You can also try to make a map yourself.

www.nationalgeographic.com/kids-world-atlas/maps.html
This National Geographic page is full of links to information about maps. The resources listed here will help you create your own maps, find maps for school reports, zoom in on different parts of the world, and much more!

www.rethinkingschools.org/just_fun/games/mapgame2.shtml
Test your knowledge of some of the world's countries! This game asks you to click and drag the correct country name to the correct place on the map. The countries are all in North Africa and the Middle East.

www.worldatlas.com/webimage/testmaps/maps.htm
On this web site, there is a section called Map Tests. You can print out lots of different maps, each one asking you to try to name the countries. The answers are given on a separate web page!

Index